TRAILS WEST

D1400043

KANSAS CITY PUBLIC LIBRARY
JUL 1 8 2013

Want to know
history

Pirates

Suzan Boshouwers & Marjolein Hund

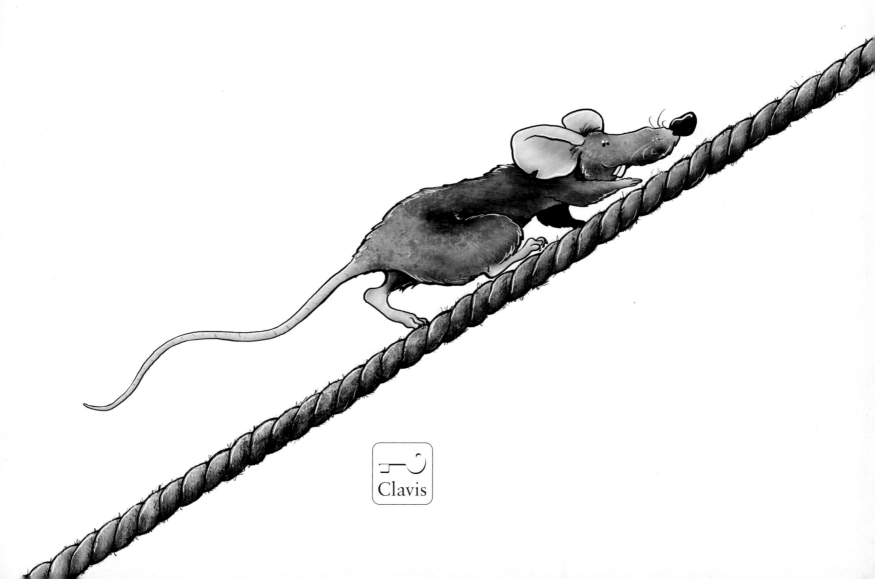

Clavis

We go on raids to plunder precious treasure!
We dream of chests filled to the brim with jewels and
pearls as big as cannonballs! Your cargo is no longer safe.
We are the terror of the high seas. Brace yourselves;
here we come!

The First Pirates

Pirates have existed for over four thousand years. They have been around as long as there have been ships with precious cargo sailing the high seas. My crew and I use a sailing ship, but the first pirate crafts were rafts made from wood and rope. These rafts moved very fast and were small enough to hide in places with shallow water and lots of rocks. There, they'd lie in wait for heavily loaded ships to sail by.

Traveling through the ocean is easier than traveling over land, which is full of high mountains and treacherous roads. Ships can carry heavy loads swiftly through the water. The West has a lot of gold and silver and the East has rice and spices. They exchange these goods with each other and a lot of this kind of trading goes on. The ocean is the perfect highway for traders.

Did you know many pirates steal from other people because they are very poor?

Did you know pirate ships can sink? That's why some people believe the bottom of the sea is covered with treasure that can be found in shipwrecks.

Belle Barnacle and I know the routes
the big loaded ships will follow.
By making raids on these ships,
we might get rich quickly. It isn't hard at all.
Dangerous pirate ships appear everywhere.
They are a real plague for sea trade.

Coconuts

Flag
The insignia of the skull and crossbones is on the pirate's flag which we call the *Jolly Roger*.

Escape route
This island has many escape routes. We keep our ship ship-shape and ready to set sail at a moment's notice.

Spyglass
Someone always keeps watch.

Fire

Preparing for the Voyage

Pirate clothes

It can be very cold at sea and pirates have to be able to move around rapidly. That's why we wear thick, short canvas jackets, linen shirts, and wide-legged cotton pants. Most of us don't wear shoes because we can slip on the ship's deck too easily. Our brightly-colored bandanas protect us against the burning sun or frosty winds, and we can use them as napkins, too! We often wear brightly-colored beads, earrings, and black eye patches.

It is considered bad luck for girls to be on board a pirate ship. That's why girl pirates dress up as boys. Can you figure out which pirate is a girl?

Provisions

We fill our bottles and jars with clean water. Sea water is too salty for anyone to drink. We keep our grub—that means our food— in watertight barrels.

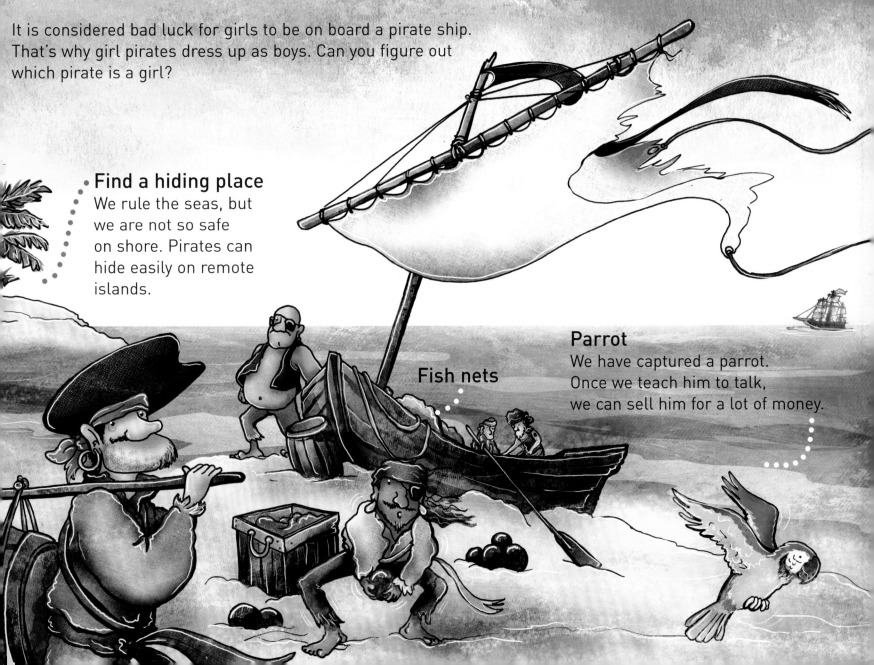

Find a hiding place
We rule the seas, but we are not so safe on shore. Pirates can hide easily on remote islands.

Fish nets

Parrot
We have captured a parrot. Once we teach him to talk, we can sell him for a lot of money.

Did you know a ship's captain has his own cabin? That's a room with a fancy chair, a table, and a bed.

The Captain

There's only one boss on a ship: the captain. That's me, Captain Billy Silver! I make sure we're all safe and I make all the important decisions. I choose the direction we're going to sail and give the sign to attack another ship. There's a lot of work that needs to be done on a ship and it's important everyone works together. That's why I give commands and special orders to my crew.

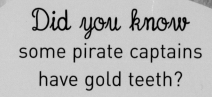

Did you know some pirate captains have gold teeth?

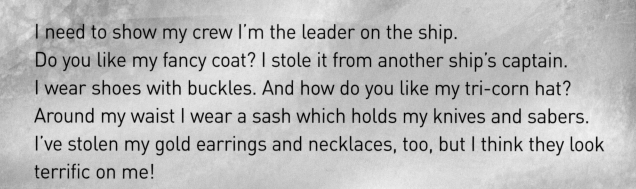

I need to show my crew I'm the leader on the ship.
Do you like my fancy coat? I stole it from another ship's captain.
I wear shoes with buckles. And how do you like my tri-corn hat?
Around my waist I wear a sash which holds my knives and sabers.
I've stolen my gold earrings and necklaces, too, but I think they look terrific on me!

Keeping Watch

At night, we take turns keeping watch on deck. You must never fall asleep when you're on lookout duty! By the way, sleeping isn't so easy on a ship. The crew sleep in hammocks, which sway from side to side all the time. It can also get very warm because the hammocks hang close to one another down in the belly of the ship. Sometimes we get bored during our long voyages and that's when we play all kinds of games, sing loud pirate songs, and teach our parrots to talk!

Pirates' lives depend on the weather. When there's no wind, our ship doesn't move. And when it's storming, the ship can get wrecked against rocks. We have to pay attention to when it's low and high tide, the wind direction, waves, dangerous cliffs...

Did you know some pirates believe there are such things as *ghost ships*?

To understand where we are,
we look at the stars to help guide us.
That's called *getting our bearings*.
Being lost at sea isn't fun, especially
when you're far from land and don't
have much grub or drink on board.

Did you know
pirates have to be nimble?
They're always climbing,
crawling, looking out, fighting,
running, hoisting the sails, or
swabbing (cleaning) the decks.

Captain Blackbeard's Glossary

Captain Blackbeard wanted to be the most famous and dangerous pirate who ever lived. With his four ships, he made the seas unsafe for traders. His real name was Edward Teach, but that didn't sound frightening enough, so he changed his name. Captain Blackbeard had fierce eyes, an enormous tangled beard, and when he attacked, clouds of smoke came out of his ears! He spoke in pirate lingo. Do you know how to speak pirate lingo?

bell

helm

captain's
cabin

galley

hammocks

Come Aboard Our Pirate Ship!

When we see a ship that we want to attack, we set off in hot pursuit. We hoist a simple nautical flag to keep it a secret that we're pirates. That way the other ship thinks everything is fine and can't prepare for our attack.

Did you know pirates throw sand on deck to stop it from being so slippery?

spyglass

lookout

nautical flag

monster figurehead

barrels (with provisions)

Who Crews on a Pirate Ship?

I am **Captain** and I decide when we attack. Avast! It won't be long!

First mate Belle Barnacle helps the ship to run in ship-shape condition. The first mate divides any loot and makes sure everyone gets equal portions of grub and drink.

The carpenter is responsible for repairing the ship. He fixes holes when the ship is damaged during an attack or a storm. The carpenter also makes ropes and sails.

The gunner fires the cannons and launches smoke bombs (containers filled with burning tar and rags).

The doctor takes care of anyone who's sick. The doctor can also fix teeth. Pirates don't clean their teeth very often!

The ship's boy is a pirate who's still learning the profession. He does all kinds of jobs, such as cleaning the captain's cabin, helping the cook, and swabbing the deck. The smallest ship's boy climbs up into the crow's nest at the top of the mast to keep a lookout.

The cook prepares our grub. Almost every day we eat hardtack biscuits, salted meat, and dried peas.

Pirate musicians entertain us during our long voyages. When we attack, it's their job to make as much noise as possible to frighten our opponents. They drum, fiddle, blow horns, and jump around screaming and hollering!

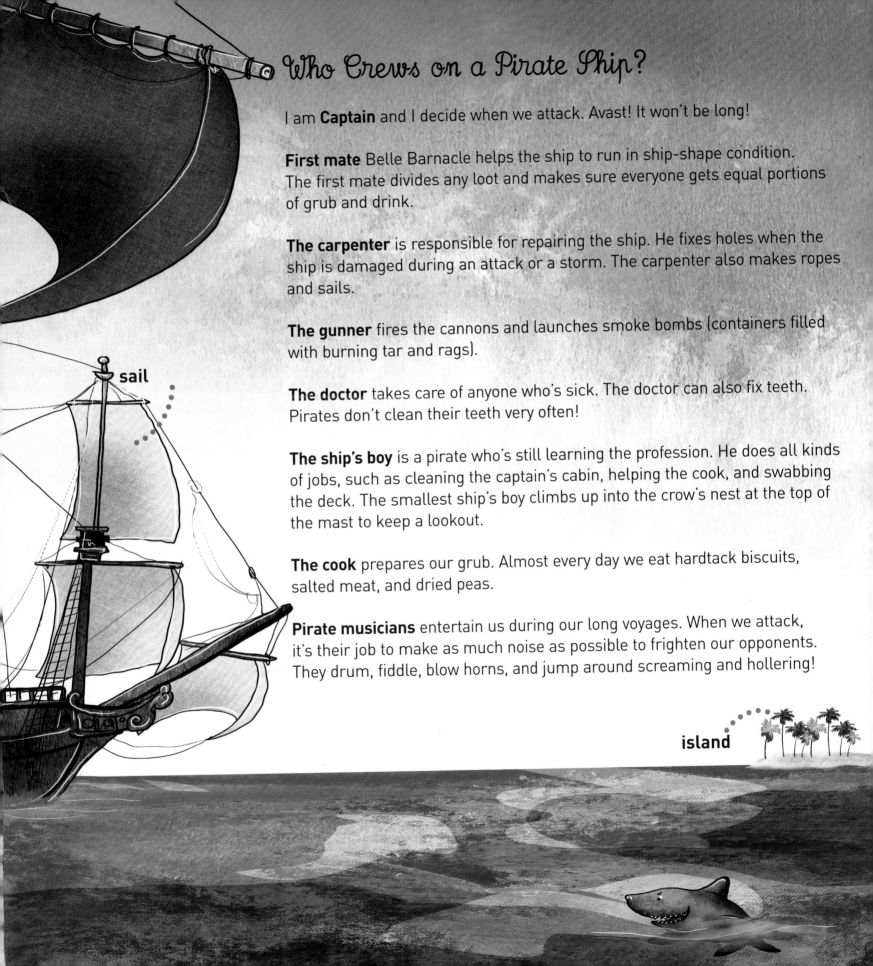

sail

island

Pirate Attack!

When I signal the crew, we hoist the Jolly Roger. It tells the other ship we're pirates. We sail swiftly towards our victim. The gunner launches smoke bombs onto their deck and fires the cannons. *What a noise!* Usually the ship we're attacking is so heavily loaded down with cargo that it doesn't have time to turn around and sail away.

Then we sail alongside the ship. We tie our ship and the enemy's ship together with thick tarred ropes. Their ship cannot drift away now. Lickety-split, we apply a gang plank and board the other ship! That's called *boarding* and from then on, we command their ship. We take the captain as our hostage and tie up their crew below deck. Then we plunder and steal everything we can. If we're lucky, we find a chest filled with silver and gold. Or even more!

When Pirates Go Ashore

Pirates always prefer to stay on their ship, but some sea voyages can take so long that after a successful raid, we like to come ashore for a little while. We divide the loot we've plundered so everyone gets their fair share. The bravest pirates get a bit more than the others, and the captain gets the most, of course!

At marketplaces where lots of pirates come, we all trade loot. We eat and drink freshly baked bread and fruit juices—things we don't have on board. We can't remain ashore for too long, so we buy new provisions such as hardtack biscuits, dried peas, salted meat, medicine, and ropes to prepare for our next voyage.

Did you know pirates like to party when they go ashore? After a successful raid, they want to celebrate their victory.

How Pirates Say Goodbye

This has been the story of my life as a pirate. I hope you had a good time at sea and on board my ship. It's not safe for pirates to stay ashore too long; we belong at sea. So, tonight we haul anchor and set sail again. Come sing along with our pirate song!

Come with us—
with the north wind,
with the south wind,
with the west wind,
with the east wind.

Come with us—
on the calm sea,
on the rolling sea,
on the quiet sea,
on the dangerous sea.
Bring us riches, gold, and luck!

Come with us—
across the horizon,
under the moon and the stars
that tell us where we are.

We hoist the sails!
We push off!
Come with us!

Fair winds!

Play a Pirate Game

Captain Billy Silver has told you everything about the life of a pirate in the olden days. As you know, pirates used to get bored during their long voyages. That's why they invented games. Games that you can play, too, like this one:

Pirates played this game with coins or pieces of gold, but you can use pebbles or small stones. Two players are needed for this game. First, draw a game board that looks like the one in the illustration on this page. Next, each player takes two pebbles and puts one at the edge of the games' board in the largest circle closest to each player. Each player hides the other pebble in one of their hands. Taking turns, each player guesses which hand the pebble's in. If you guess incorrectly, you don't do anything. If you guess correctly, you put your own pebble in a circle one circle in towards the center of the game board. The first player to place their pebble in the middle X wins.

Tip: If you're at the beach, you can draw the pirate game board in the sand.

Storm!

What a storm! All the pirates' hats, caps, and bandanas have blown off their heads! Do you know on whose head each covering belongs? Hurry, before they all land in the ocean!

Pirate-quiz

1. What's a pirate?

2. Why do pirates take fresh water on their ships?

3. What do pirates do when they are bored during long voyages?

4. What do pirates look for when they rob ships?

5. What's the leader of a pirate ship called?

6. What does "boarding" mean?

7. What do pirates do when they are ashore?

8. What does a ship's boy have to do?

9. Why is it so important to have a carpenter on board?

10. Why would pirates hoist a nautical flag and not their Jolly Roger?